HEALTH—
A GIFT OF GOD

by
Billy B. Smith

Printed in the United States of America.

Billy B. Smith Ministries Publications
P.O. Box 6078
Ft. Worth, Texas 76115 U.S.A.

ISBN 1-879612-02-X

ACKNOWLEDGEMENTS

It would be impossible to write a book like this without the help and encouragement of those around you. To all those who helped and encouraged me to complete this book, I would like to say thank you.

I would like to give special thanks to:

My wife, Mary, and our two children, Billy Wayne and Amy, for their patience and understanding during these long weeks of writing.

Catherine Skipper of Great Yarmouth, England for over two hundred hours of scripture searching and writing. Without her help, this book could not have been completed.

INTRODUCTION

I have written this book for people who have sickness or disease in their bodies.

Hosea 4:6

My people are destroyed for lack of knowledge.
(Another version of the Bible says, "They die for lack of knowledge.")

If you do not know God is a healer, you do not go to God for healing. If you think God is punishing you with sickness, you do not go to God for healing. If you think God wants to heal some people but not others, your case will always be the one God does not heal.

All of these ideas come because of a lack of knowledge about God and His will.

John 8:31-32

Jesus said, *"If you abide in My word, then you are truly disciples of Mine; and you shall know the truth, and the truth shall make you free."*

God is not moved by our needs. God is only moved by our faith in His Word.

Romans 10:17

Faith comes from hearing, and hearing by the word of Christ.

We must hear God's Word over and over to build our faith to the point of receiving from God. That is why you must read this book—out loud—to yourself, over and over. **Faith does not come from reading alone; it comes from hearing and hearing God's Word.**

This book will not take the place of your own Bible reading, but I have helped you to center on one part of God's will for your life—**HEALTH!**

Remember, when you read the Word, read it out loud so you can hear the Word over and over. This will cause faith to be produced in you. I want to especially encourage those who are sick and have not been able to receive their healing, as well as those who have incurable diseases, to read this book out loud. **It will cause your faith to rise up so you can receive your healing.**

For those who cannot read or are too sick to read, we have a cassette tape of this message. You may order this tape by writing to:

Billy Smith Ministries
P.O. Box 6078
Ft. Worth, TX 76115 U.S.A

HEALTH—
A Gift of God

Father, in the name of Jesus we come before You and we pray for those who are reading this book. Father, Your Word is life, and in the name of Jesus, I command them to hear and see. I loose their eyes and their ears that they might see and hear Your Word. You said that if they saw and they heard, they would receive. So Father, let them receive Your Word now in the fullness of its power, in the name of Jesus.

Genesis 17:1

When Abram was ninety-nine years old, the Lord appeared to Abram and said to him, "I am God Almighty; walk before Me, and be blameless."

When the Lord God appeared to Abram, what He actually said, in Hebrew, was "I am El Shaddai." *El Shaddai* is one of seven covenant names used to describe God and His power to Israel. In Hebrew, *El Shaddai* means "The All-sufficient One" or "The God Who Is More Than Enough."

All through the Old and New Testament, El Shaddai, the Almighty God, has revealed and unveiled himself as the God who is more than enough.

Most of us believe God is able to do the mighty works spoken of in the Bible, but we find it hard to believe He will do them for us.

We must see that it is God's will for you and me to walk in the promises of God. When we were born again by accepting Jesus as our Savior (according to Romans 10:9-10), we became sons and daughters of God. He has now become **our** Heavenly Father. Because of this, He says that He loves us more than our earthly fathers. He loves us so much that He gave His only son that we could be made **complete in Jesus.**

Most people believe that God could do these mighty works spoken of in the Bible, but to dare think He would do them for us is a different story. That would be presumptuous. Why would God even think about us?

Well, I will tell you why. He created us and we are now His children. Luke 9:55-56 indicates that He is motivated by a different spirit. He is motivated by the spirit of love. He says He loves us more than our earthly fathers. No earthly father would want anything but the best for his children, and **God certainly is no different.**

John 3:16

"For God so loved the world, that He gave His only begotten Son, that whoever be-

lieves in Him should not perish, but have eternal life."

1 John 4:14
We have beheld and bear witness that the Father has sent the Son to be the Savior of the world.

When we look up the word *salvation*, we find it means "to be made whole or complete—physically, spiritually, and mentally (body, soul, and spirit).

There was no one name that could describe God, so there were several names used in the Bible to describe the attributes of God.

He was known as:

Jehovah-Tisidkenu—God Our Righteousness

2 Corinthians 5:21
He made Him who knew no sin to be sin on our behalf, that we might become the righteousness of God in Him.

Jehovah-M'kaddesh—God Who Sanctifies
He not only made us righteous but has **cleansed** us and made us holy.

Jehovah-Shalom—God Is Our Peace

Isaiah 53:5 (KJV)
The chastisement of our peace was upon him.

Jesus bore that which was needful for our peace.

Jehovah-Shammah—God Is There

Hebrews 13:5 (KJV)
>Jesus said, *I will never leave thee, nor forsake thee.*

Jehovah-Jireh—God Who Provides

Philippians 4:19 (KJV)
>*God shall supply all your need according to his riches in glory by Christ Jesus.*

Jehovah-Nissi—God Our Victory and Banner

Romans 8:37 (KJV)
>*In all these things we are more than conquerors through him that loved us.*

Jehovah-Rophe—God Our Healer

Exodus 15:26 (KJV)
>*I am the Lord that healeth thee.*

John 10:30
>Jesus said, *"I and the Father are one."*

They are in agreement. They think the same way. They do the same things. If God is a healer, then Jesus is a healer.

John, chapter one, says that God and the Word are the same and that Jesus is the Word.

Psalm 107:20
*He **sent His word** and healed them, and delivered them from their destructions.*

Hebrews 13:8
Jesus Christ is the same yesterday and today, yes and forever.

John 10:10
"The thief [Satan] *comes only to steal, and kill, and destroy; I came that they might have life, and might have it abundantly."*

Abundant life is not sickness, disease, or pain.

James 1:17
Every good thing bestowed and every perfect gift is from above, coming down from the Father of lights, with whom there is no variation, or shifting shadow.

Acts 10:34 (KJV)
Peter said, *Of a truth I perceive that God is no respecter of persons.*

It Is God's Will For All To Be Healed
I don't believe we could find a better scripture describing the will of God than...

3 John 2 (KJV)

Beloved, I wish above all things (not above some things, but above all things) *that thou mayest prosper and be in health, even as thy soul prospereth.*

Isaiah 53:5

But He was pierced through for our trans-gressions, He was crushed for our iniqui-ties; the chastening for our well-being fell upon Him, and by His scourging we are healed.

Exodus 23:25

"But you shall serve the Lord your God, and He will bless your bread and your water, and I will remove sickness from your midst."

Psalm 103:1-5

Bless the Lord, O my soul; and all that is within me, bless His holy name. Bless the Lord, O my soul, and forget none of His benefits **(You mean there are benefits in serving God? Yes, I do. Listen!)** *Who pardons all your iniquities; **who heals all your diseases;** who redeems your life from the pit; **who crowns you with lovingkind-ness and compassion;** who satisfies your years with good things, so that your youth is renewed like the eagle.*

Jesus never refused to heal anyone. His healing power was available to anyone who would receive it. It is a gift, and we must accept it for ourselves. It is a gift, and we must reach out and take hold of it.

Mark 1:39-42

He went into their synagogues throughout all Galilee, preaching and casting out the demons. And a leper came to Him, beseeching Him and falling on his knees before Him, and saying to Him, "If You are willing, You can make me clean." And moved with compassion, He stretched out His hand, and touched him, and said to him, "I am willing; be cleansed." And immediately the leprosy left him and he was cleansed.

Matthew 9:35

Jesus was going about all the cities and the villages, teaching in their synagogues, and proclaiming the gospel of the kingdom, and healing every kind of disease and every kind of sickness.

Did you hear that? Every kind of disease and every kind of sickness. There was no one He did not reach out and heal.

Luke 6:19

All the multitude were trying to touch Him, for power was coming from Him and healing them all.

Psalm 103:3

Who pardons all your iniquities; who heals all your diseases.

Jeremiah 30:17

"'For I will restore you to health and I will heal you of your wounds,' declares the Lord."

If it is God's will to heal everyone, then why isn't everyone healed?

Mark 16:15-16 tells us that we as believers are to go and preach the gospel. As we preach the gospel, some will believe, but some will not. Those who will believe will be born again; those who will not will be damned.

Matthew 13:54-58

Coming to His home town He began teaching them in their synagogue, so that they became astonished, and said, "Where did this man get this wisdom, and these miraculous powers? Is not this the carpenter's son? Is not His mother called Mary, and His brothers, James and Joseph and Simon and Judas? And His sisters, are they not all with us? Where then did this man get all these things?" And they took offense at Him. But Jesus said to them, "A prophet is not without honor except in his home town, and in his own household." And He did not do many miracles there because of their unbelief.

In some versions of the Bible, it says, "He could do no mighty miracles because of the hardness of their hearts." They refused to believe.

The people of His own village would not believe the things that were going on in every village, in every city, in every town around His home town. The Bible says for the hardness of their hearts they refused to believe. I want you to notice that it says He had wisdom. They recognized His miraculous power but refused to believe what He said.

The main reason I find for not being healed is in...

Hosea 4:6
*My people are **destroyed** for **lack** of knowledge.*

For there to be a lack of knowledge, there must be knowledge. God has given this to us in His Word.

Psalm 107:20
He sent His word and healed them, and delivered them from their destructions.

Proverbs 4:20-22

*My son, give attention to my **words**; incline your ear to my sayings. Do not let them depart from your sight; keep them in the midst of your heart. For they are life to those who find them, and health to all their whole body.*

The words of God are health to the whole body.

Hebrews 11:1

Now faith is the assurance of things hoped for, the conviction of things not seen.

Hebrews 11:6

Without faith it is impossible to please Him, for he who comes to God must believe that He is, and that He is a rewarder of those who seek Him.

1 John 5:4

For whatever is born of God overcomes the world; and this is the victory that has overcome the world—our faith.

Romans 10:17

So faith comes from hearing, and hearing by the word of Christ.

You will notice this says that *faith comes by hearing.* It does not say that faith comes by strictly reading, but we must *hear* the Word of God. As we hear it, it goes into our spirits. So listen to the Word of God as you read, and receive it into your spirit.

Matthew 9:20-22

And behold, a woman who had been suffering from a hemorrhage for twelve years, came up behind Him and touched the fringe of His cloak; for she was saying to herself, "If I only touch His garment, I shall get well." But Jesus turning and seeing her said, "Daughter, take courage; your faith has made you well."

Matthew 9:28-29

After He had come into the house, the blind men came up to Him, and Jesus said to them, "Do you believe that I am able to do this?" They said to Him, "Yes, Lord." Then He touched their eyes, saying, "Be it done to you according to your faith."

Mark 9:23

And Jesus said to him, "'If you can [believe]!' *All things are possible to him who believes."*

Believing in healing is not enough. You must see that it is God's will to heal all who come to Him. He sees us as already healed, according to His Word. He does not deny our symptoms, but according to His Word and because of the price Jesus paid,

He refuses our bodies the right to stay sick. Healing is a gift and we must accept it. God will not force it on us.

1 Peter 2:24

He Himself bore our sins in His body on the cross, that we might die to sin and live to righteousness; for by His wounds you were healed.

James 5:14-15

Is anyone among you sick? Let him call for the elders of the church, and let them pray over him, anointing him with oil in the name of the Lord; and the prayer offered in faith will restore the one who is sick, and the Lord will raise him up, and if he has committed sins, they will be forgiven him.

Did you notice it says, "Is there anyone among you sick?" There should not be, but if there is, call for the elders of the Church.

God is no respecter of people and He cannot lie. Since He is the same yesterday, today, and forever, if He has ever healed anyone, then you can also expect God's mercy and grace to touch your body. Every time you hear about God healing someone, you can lay claim to this promise for your body.

Matthew 4:23-24

And Jesus was going about in all Galilee, teaching in their synagogues, and proclaim-

ing the gospel of the kingdom, and healing every kind of disease and every kind of sickness among the people. And the news about Him went out into all Syria; and they brought to Him all who were ill, taken with various diseases and pains, demoniacs, epileptics, paralytics; and He healed them.

Matthew 8:2-10, 13-17

And behold, a leper came to Him, and bowed down to Him, saying, "Lord, if You are willing, You can make me clean." And He stretched out His hand and touched him, saying, "I am willing; be cleansed." And immediately his leprosy was cleansed. And Jesus said to him, "See that you tell no one; but go, show yourself to the priest, and present the offering that Moses commanded, for a testimony to them.

And when He had entered Capernaum, a centurion came to Him, entreating Him, and saying, "Lord, my servant is lying paralyzed at home, suffering great pain." And He said to him, "I will come and heal him." But the centurion answered and said, "Lord, I am not worthy for You to come under my roof, but just say the word, and my servant will be healed. For I, too, am a man under authority, with soldiers under me; and I say to this one, 'Go!' and he goes, and to another, 'Come!' and he

*comes, and to my slave, 'Do this!' and he
does it."*

*Now when Jesus heard this, He marveled,
and said to those who were following,
"Truly I say to you, I have not found such
great faith with anyone in Israel. And Jesus
said to the centurion, "Go your way; let it
be done to you as you have believed." And
the servant was healed that very hour.*

*And when Jesus had come to Peter's home,
He saw his mother-in-law lying sick in bed
with a fever. And He touched her hand, and
the fever left her; and she arose, and waited
on Him. And when evening had come, they
brought to Him many who were demon-possessed; and He cast out the spirits with a
word, and healed all who were ill in order
that what was spoken through Isaiah the
prophet might be fulfilled, saying, "HE
HIMSELF TOOK OUR INFIRMITIES,
AND CARRIED AWAY OUR DISEASES."*

Matthew 9:2-8

*And behold, they were bringing to Him a
paralytic, lying on a bed; and Jesus seeing
their faith said to the paralytic, "Take
courage, My son, your sins are forgiven."
And behold, some of the scribes said to
themselves, "This fellow blasphemes." And
Jesus knowing their thoughts said, "Why
are you thinking evil in your hearts? For
which is easier, to say, 'Your sins are forgiv-*

20

en,' or to say, 'Rise, and walk'? But in order that you may know that the Son of Man has authority on earth to forgive sins"—then He said to the paralytic— "Rise, take up your bed, and go home." And he rose, and went home. But when the multitudes saw this, they were filled with awe, and glorified God, who had given such authority to men.

Matthew 9:18-26

While He was saying these things to them, behold, there came a synagogue official, and bowed down before Him, saying, "My daughter has just died; but come and lay Your hand on her, and she will live." And Jesus rose and began to follow him, and so did His disciples.

And behold, a woman who had been suffering from a hemorrhage for twelve years, came up behind Him and touched the fringe of His cloak; for she was saying to herself, "If I only touch His garment, I shall get well." But Jesus turning and seeing her said, "Daughter, take courage; your faith has made you well." And at once the woman was made well.

And when Jesus came into the official's house, and saw the flute-players, and the crowd in noisy disorder, He began to say, "Depart; for the girl has not died, but is asleep." And they began laughing at Him.

But when the crowd had been put out, He entered and took her by the hand; and the girl arose. And this news went out into all that land.

Matthew 9:32-33

And as they were going out, behold, a dumb man, demon-possessed, was brought to Him. And after the demon was cast out, the dumb man spoke; and the multitudes marveled, saying, "Nothing like this was ever seen in Israel."

Matthew 9:35

And Jesus was going about all the cities and the villages, teaching in their synagogues, and proclaiming the gospel of the kingdom, and healing every kind of disease and every kind of sickness.

Matthew 10:1

And having summoned His twelve disciples, He gave them authority over unclean spirits, to cast them out, and to heal every kind of disease and every kind of sickness.

Matthew 10:7-8

"And as you go, preach, saying, 'The kingdom of heaven is at hand.' Heal the sick, raise the dead, cleanse the lepers, cast out demons; freely you received, freely give."

Matthew 12:10-15

And behold, there was a man with a withered hand. And they questioned Him, saying, "Is it lawful to heal on the Sabbath?"— in order that they might accuse Him. And He said to them, "What man shall there be among you, who shall have one sheep, and if it falls into a pit on the Sabbath, will he not take hold of it, and lift it out? Of how much more value then is a man than a sheep! So then, it is lawful to do good on the Sabbath." Then He said to the man, "Stretch out your hand!" And he stretched it out, and it was restored to normal, like the other. But the Pharisees went out, and counseled together against Him, as to how they might destroy Him. But Jesus, aware of this, withdrew from there. And many followed Him, and He healed them all.

Matthew 12:22-23

Then there was brought to Him a demon-possessed man who was blind and dumb, and He healed him, so that the dumb man spoke and saw. And all the multitudes were amazed, and began to say, "This man cannot be the Son of David, can He?"

Matthew 14:35-36

And when the men of that place recognized Him, they sent into all that surrounding district and brought to Him all who were sick;

and they began to entreat Him that they might just touch the fringe of His cloak; and as many as touched it were cured.

Matthew 15:22-31

And behold, a Canaanite woman came out from that region, and began to cry out, saying, "Have mercy on me, O Lord, Son of David; my daughter is cruelly demon-possessed." But He did not answer her a word. And His disciples came to Him and kept asking Him, saying, "Send her away, for she is shouting out after us." But He answered and said, "I was sent only to the lost sheep of the house of Israel." But she came and began to bow down before Him, saying, "Lord, help me!" And He answered and said, "It is not good to take the children's bread and throw it to the dogs." But she said, "Yes, Lord; but even the dogs feed on the crumbs which fall from their master's table." Then Jesus answered and said to her, "O woman, your faith is great; be it done for you as you wish." And her daughter was healed at once.

And departing from there, Jesus went along by the Sea of Galilee, and having gone up to the mountain, He was sitting there. And great multitudes came to Him, bringing with them those who were lame, crippled, blind, dumb, and many others, and they laid them down at His feet; and He healed them, so

*that the multitude marveled as they saw the
dumb speaking, the crippled restored, and
the lame walking, and the blind seeing; and
they glorified the God of Israel.*

Matthew 17:14-18

*And when they came to the multitude, a man
came up to Him, falling on his knees before
Him, and saying, "Lord, have mercy on my
son, for he is a lunatic, and is very ill; for
he often falls into the fire, and often into the
water. And I brought him to Your disciples,
and they could not cure him." And Jesus
answered and said, "O unbelieving and
perverted generation, how long shall I be
with you? How long shall I put up with
you? Bring him here to Me." And Jesus
rebuked him, and the demon came out of
him, and the boy was cured at once.*

Isaiah 54:13-14

*"And all your sons will be taught of the
Lord; and the well-being of your sons will
be great. In righteousness you will be
established; you will be far from oppres-
sion, for you will not fear; and from terror,
for it will not come near you."*

Isaiah 54:17

*"No weapon that is formed against you
shall prosper; and every tongue that accus-
es you in judgment you will condemn."*

Matthew 24:35

"Heaven and earth will pass away, but My words shall not pass away."

Psalm 119:114 (AMP)

You are my hiding place and my shield; I hope in Your Word.

Isaiah 40:8

The grass withers, the flower fades, but the word of our God stands forever.

Proverbs 4:20-22

My son, give attention to my words; incline your ear to my sayings. Do not let them depart from your sight; keep them in the midst of your heart. For they are life to those who find them, and health to their whole body.

We must remember that God is no respecter of persons. If we will take the Word of God, and place it in our hearts and keep it before us day and night, it will become health to our whole body.

Mark 1:30-34

Now Simon's mother-in-law was lying sick with a fever; and immediately they spoke to Him about her. And He came to her and raised her up, taking her by the hand, and the fever left her, and she waited on them.

And when evening had come, after the sun had set, they began bringing to Him all who were ill and those who were demon-possessed. And the whole city had gathered at the door. And He healed many who were ill with various diseases, and cast out many demons; and He was not permitting the demons to speak, because they knew who He was.

Mark 1:39-42

And He went into their synagogues throughout all Galilee, preaching and casting out the demons. And a leper came to Him, beseeching Him and falling on his knees before Him, and saying to Him, "If You are willing, You can make me clean." And moved with compassion, He stretched out His hand, and touched him, and said to him, "I am willing; be cleansed." And immediately the leprosy left him and he was cleansed.

Mark 2:3-12

And they came, bringing to Him a paralytic, carried by four men. And being unable to get to Him because of the crowd, they removed the roof above Him; and when they had dug an opening, they let down the pallet on which the paralytic was lying. And Jesus seeing their faith said to the paralytic, "My son, your sins are forgiven."

But there were some of the scribes sitting there and reasoning in their hearts, "Why does this man speak that way? He is blaspheming; who can forgive sins but God alone?" And immediately Jesus, aware in His spirit that they were reasoning that way within themselves, said to them, "Why are you reasoning about these things in your hearts? Which is easier, to say to the paralytic, 'Your sins are forgiven'; or to say, 'Arise, and take up your pallet and walk'? But in order that you may know that the Son of Man has authority on earth to forgive sins"—He said to the paralytic, "I say to you, rise, take up your pallet and go home." And he rose and immediately took up the pallet and went out in the sight of all; so that they were all amazed and were glorifying God, saying, "We have never seen anything like this."

Mark 3:1-5

And He entered again into a synagogue; and a man was there with a withered hand. And they were watching Him to see if He would heal him on the Sabbath, in order that they might accuse Him. And He said to the man with the withered hand, "Rise and come forward!" And He said to them, "Is it lawful on the Sabbath to do good or to do harm, to save a life or to kill?" But they kept silent. And after looking around at

*them with anger, grieved at their hardness
of heart, He said to the man, "Stretch out
your hand." And he stretched it out, and
his hand was restored.*

Mark 3:10-11

*For He had healed many, with the result
that all those who had afflictions pressed
about Him in order to touch Him. And
whenever the unclean spirits beheld Him,
they would fall down before Him and cry
out, saying, "You are the Son of God!"*

Mark 3:14-15

*And He appointed twelve, that they might be
with Him, and that He might send them out
to preach, and to have authority to cast out
the demons.*

Mark 5:22-43

*And one of the synagogue officials named
Jairus came up, and upon seeing Him, fell
at His feet, and entreated Him earnestly,
saying, "My little daughter is at the point of
death; please come and lay Your hands on
her, that she may get well and live." And
He went off with him; and a great multitude
was following Him and pressing in on Him.
And a woman who had had a hemorrhage
for twelve years, and had endured much at
the hands of many physicians, and had
spent all that she had and was not helped at*

*all, but rather had grown worse, after hear-
ing about Jesus, came up in the crowd
behind Him, and touched His cloak. For
she thought, "If I just touch His garments, I
shall get well." And immediately the flow
of her blood was dried up; and she felt in
her body that she was healed of her affliction.*

*And immediately Jesus, perceiving in Him-
self that the power proceeding from Him
had gone forth, turned around in the crowd
and said, "Who touched My garments?"
And His disciples said to Him, "You see the
multitude pressing in on You, and You say,
'Who touched Me?'"*

*And He looked around to see the woman
who had done this. But the woman fearing
and trembling, aware of what had happened
to her, came and fell down before Him, and
told Him the whole truth. And He said to
her, "Daughter, your faith has made you
well; go in peace, and be healed of your
affliction."*

*While He was still speaking, they came from
the house of the synagogue official, saying,
"Your daughter has died; why trouble the
Teacher anymore?" But Jesus, overhearing
what was being spoken, said to the synagogue official, **"Do not be afraid any
longer, only believe."** And He allowed no
one to follow with Him, except Peter and
James and John the brother of James. And*

*they came to the house of the synagogue
official; and He beheld a commotion, and
people loudly weeping and wailing. And
entering in, He said to them, "Why make a
commotion and weep? The child has not
died, but is asleep." And they began laughing at Him. But putting them all out, He
took along the child's father and mother and
His own companions, and entered the room
where the child was.*

*And taking the child by the hand, He said
to her, "Talitha kum!" (which translated
means, "Little girl, I say to you, arise!")
And immediately the girl rose and began to
walk; for she was twelve years old. And
immediately they were completely astound-
ed. And He gave them strict orders that no
one should know about this; and He said
that something should be given her to eat.*

Mark 6:7

*And He summoned the twelve and began to
send them out in pairs; and He was giving
them authority over the unclean spirits.*

Mark 6:12-13

*And they went out and preached that men
should repent. And they were casting out
many demons and were anointing with oil
many sick people and healing them.*

Mark 6:53-56

*And when they had crossed over they came
to land at Gennesaret, and moored to the
shore. And when they had come out of the
boat, immediately the people recognized
Him, and ran about that whole country and
began to carry about on their pallets those
who were sick, to the place they heard He
was. And wherever He entered villages, or
cities, or countryside, they were laying the
sick in the market places, and entreating
Him that they might just touch the fringe of
His cloak; and as many as touched it were
being cured.*

Mark 7:25-30

*But after hearing of Him, a woman whose
little daughter had an unclean spirit, immediately came and fell at His feet. Now
the woman was a Gentile, of the Syro-
phoenician race. And she kept asking Him
to cast the demon out of her daughter. And
He was saying to her, "Let the children be
satisfied first, for it is not good to take the
children's bread and throw it to the dogs."
But she answered and said to Him, "Yes,
Lord, but even the dogs under the table feed
on the children's crumbs." And He said to
her, "Because of this answer go your way;
the demon has gone out of your daughter."
And going back to her home, she found the*

child lying on the bed, the demon having departed.

Mark 7:32-37

And they brought to Him one who was deaf and spoke with difficulty, and they entreated Him to lay His hand upon him. And He took him aside from the multitude by himself, and put His fingers into his ears, and after spitting, He touched his tongue with the saliva; and looking up to heaven with a deep sigh, He said to him, "Ephphatha!" that is, "Be opened!" And his ears were opened, and the impediment of his tongue was removed, and he began speaking plainly. And He gave them orders not to tell anyone; but the more He ordered them, the more widely they continued to proclaim it. And they were utterly astonished, saying, "He has done all things well; He makes even the deaf to hear, and the dumb to speak."

Mark 8:22-25

And they came to Bethsaida. And they brought a blind man to Him, and entreated Him to touch him. And taking the blind man by the hand, He brought him out of the village; and after spitting on his eyes, and laying His hands upon him, He asked him, "Do you see anything?" And he looked up and said, "I see men, for I am seeing them

*like trees, walking about." Then again He
laid His hands upon his eyes; and he looked
intently and was restored, and began to see
everything clearly.*

Mark 9:14-27

*And when they came back to the disciples,
they saw a large crowd around them, and
some scribes arguing with them. And
immediately, when the entire crowd saw
Him, they were amazed, and began running
up to greet Him. And He asked them,
"What are you discussing with them?" And
one of the crowd answered Him, "Teacher, I
brought You my son, possessed with a spirit
which makes him mute; and whenever it
seizes him, it dashes him to the ground and
he foams at the mouth, and grinds his teeth,
and stiffens out. And I told Your disciples to
cast it out, and they could not do it." And
He answered them and said, "O unbelieving
generation, how long shall I be with you?
How long shall I put up with you? Bring
him to Me."*

*And they brought the boy to Him. And when
he saw Him, immediately the spirit threw
him into a convulsion, and falling to the
ground, he began rolling about and foaming
at the mouth. And He asked his father,
"How long has this been happening to
him?" And he said, "From childhood. And
it has often thrown him both into the fire*

and into the water to destroy him. But if You can do anything, take pity on us and help us!" And Jesus said to him, "'If You can [believe]*!' All things are possible to him who believes." Immediately the boy's father cried out and began saying, "I do believe; help my unbelief." And when Jesus saw that a crowd was rapidly gathering, He rebuked the unclean spirit, saying to it, "You deaf and dumb spirit, I command you, come out of him and* **do not enter him again.**" **(Did you hear that? "Do not enter him again." Nahum 1:9 (KJV) says,** *Affliction shall not rise up a second time.* **That's what Jesus was speaking of when He said, "Do not enter him again.")** *And after crying out and throwing him into terrible convulsions, it came out; and the boy became so much like a corpse that most of them said, "He is dead!" But Jesus took him by the hand and raised him; and he got up.*

Mark 10:46-52

And they came to Jericho. And as He was going out from Jericho with His disciples and a great multitude, a blind beggar named Bartimaeus, the son of Timaeus, was siting by the road. And when he heard that it was Jesus the Nazarene, he began to cry out and say, "Jesus, Son of David, have mercy on me!" And many were sternly telling him to be quiet, but he kept crying out all the more, "Son of David, have mercy on me!" And Jesus stopped and said, "Call him here." And they called the blind man, saying to him, "Take courage, arise! He is calling for you." And casting aside his cloak, he jumped up, and came to Jesus. And answering him, Jesus said, "What do you want Me to do for you?" And the blind man said to Him, "Rabboni, I want to regain my sight!" And Jesus said to him, "Go your way; your faith has made you well." And immediately he regained his sight and began following Him on the road.

Mark 16:17-18

"And these signs will accompany those who have believed: in My name they will cast out demons; they will speak with new tongues; they will pick up serpents, and if they drink any deadly poison, it shall not hurt them; they will lay hands on the sick, and **THEY WILL RECOVER.**"

Proverbs 4:20-22

My son, give attention to my **words**; incline your ear to my sayings. Do not let them depart from your sight; keep them in the midst of your heart. For they are life to those who find them, and health to all their whole body.

Hebrews 13:8

Jesus Christ is the same yesterday and today, yes and forever.

Psalm 103:1-5

Bless the Lord, O my soul; and all that is within me, bless his holy name.
Bless the Lord, O my soul, and forget none of His benefits;
*who pardons **all** your iniquities;*
*who heals **all** your diseases;*
who redeems your life from the pit;
who crowns you with lovingkindness and compassion;
*who **satisfies your years with GOOD THINGS,***
so that your youth is renewed like the eagle.

Jeremiah 30:17

"'For I will restore you to health and I will heal you of your wounds,' declares the Lord."

Psalm 107:20

He sent His word and healed them, and delivered them from their destructions.

Acts 10:34

"I most certainly understand now that God is not one to show partiality."

What He will do for anyone else, He will do for you, if you will ask Him in the Name of Jesus.

John 16:24

"Until now you have asked for nothing in My name; ask, and you will receive, that your joy may be made full."

Ask anything in the name of Jesus and He will give it to you, that your joy may be full. God wants you to have joy, and when you have sickness, there is no joy.

Luke 4:18-19

"THE SPIRIT OF THE LORD IS UPON ME, BECAUSE HE ANOINTED ME TO PREACH THE GOSPEL TO THE POOR. HE HAS SENT ME TO PROCLAIM RELEASE TO THE CAPTIVES, AND RECOVERY OF SIGHT TO THE BLIND, TO SET FREE THOSE WHO ARE DOWN-TRODDEN, TO PROCLAIM THE FAVOR-ABLE YEAR OF THE LORD."

Luke 4:31-32

And He came down to Capernaum, a city of Galilee. And He was teaching them on the Sabbath; and they were amazed at His teaching, for His message was with authority.

Luke 4:38-39

And He arose and left the synagogue, and entered Simon's home. Now Simon's mother-in-law was suffering from a high fever; and they made request of Him on her behalf. And standing over her, He rebuked the fever, and it left her; and she immediately arose and waited on them.

Luke 4:40-42

And while the sun was setting, all who had any sick with various diseases brought them to Him; and laying His hands on every one of them, He was healing them. And demons also were coming out of many, crying out and saying, "You are the Son of God!" And rebuking them, He would not allow them to speak, because they knew Him to be the Christ.

Mark 13:31

"Heaven and earth will pass away, but My words will not pass away."

Galatians 3:29

And if you belong to Christ, then you are Abraham's offspring, heirs according to promise.

Ephesians 3:6

To be specific, the Gentiles are fellow heirs and fellow members of the body, and fellow

partakers *of the promise in Christ Jesus*
through the gospel.

Because of the price Jesus paid when He hung on the cross, we have been offered the **free** gift of salvation. That gift includes forgiveness of sin, but it also means we can receive the free gift of the Holy Spirit (mentioned in Acts 2:38) and the free gifts of healing mentioned in 1 Corinthians 12:9.

This is a gift. We must understand that. **It is not forced on us,** but offered to us. We must reach out and take hold of God's promise of healing, by faith.

As you hear God's Word, reach out and receive these promises for yourself and your family.

Acts 10:34

Peter said: "I most certainly understand now that God is not one to show partiality."

Psalm 107:20

He sent His word and healed them, and delivered them from their destructions.

Luke 5:12-15

And it came about that while He was in one of the cities, behold, there was a man full of leprosy; and when He saw Jesus, he fell on his face and implored Him, saying, "Lord, if You are willing, You can make me clean." And He stretched out His hand, and touched him, saying, "I am willing; be cleansed."

And immediately the leprosy left him. And he ordered him to tell no one, "But go and show yourself to the priest, and make an offering for your cleansing, just as Moses commanded, for a testimony to them." But the news about Him was spreading even farther, and great multitudes were gathering to hear Him and to be healed of their sicknesses.

Luke 5:18-26

And behold, some men were carrying on a bed a man who was paralyzed; and they were trying to bring him in, to set him down in front of Him. And not finding any way to bring him in because of the crowd, they went up on the roof and let him down through the tiles with his stretcher, right in the center, in front of Jesus. And seeing their faith, He said, "Friend, your sins are forgiven you." And the Scribes and the Pharisees began to reason, saying, "Who is this man who speaks blasphemies? Who can forgive sins, but God alone?"

But Jesus, aware of their reasoning, answered and said to them, "Why are you reasoning in your hearts? Which is easier, to say, 'Your sins have been forgiven you,' or to say, 'Rise and walk'? But in order that you may know that the Son of Man has authority on earth to forgive sins"—He said to the paralytic—"I say to you, rise,

*and take up your stretcher and go home."
And at once he rose up before them, and
took up what he had been lying on, and
went home, glorifying God. And they were
all seized with astonishment and began glorifying God; and they were filled with fear,
saying, "We have seen remarkable things
today."*

Luke 6:6-10

*And it came about on another Sabbath, that
He entered the synagogue and was teaching; and there was a man there whose right
hand was withered. And the scribes and the
Pharisees were watching Him closely, to see
if He healed on the Sabbath, in order that
they might find reason to accuse Him. But
He knew what they were thinking, and He
said to the man with the withered hand,
"Rise and come forward!" And he rose and
came forward. And Jesus said to them, "I
ask you, is it lawful on the Sabbath to do
good, or to do harm, to save a life, or to
destroy it?" And after looking around at
them all, He said to him, "Stretch out your
hand!" And he did so; and his hand was
restored.*

Luke 6:17-19

*And He descended with them, and stood on
a level place; and there was a great multitude of His disciples, and a great throng of*

people from all Judea and Jerusalem and the coastal region of Tyre and Sidon, who had come to hear Him, and to be healed of their diseases; and those who were troubled with unclean spirits were being cured. And all the multitude were trying to touch Him, for power was coming from Him and healing them all.

Luke 7:2-10

And a certain centurion's slave, who was highly regarded by him, was sick and about to die. And when he heard about Jesus, he sent some Jewish elders asking Him to come and save the life of his slave. And when they had come to Jesus, they earnestly entreated Him, saying, "He is worthy for You to grant this to him; for he loves our nation, and it was he who built us our synagogue." Now Jesus started on His way with them; and when He was already not far from the house, the centurion sent friends, saying to Him, "Lord, do not trouble Yourself further, for I am not worthy for You to come under my roof; for this reason I did not even consider myself worthy to come to You, but just say the word, and my servant will be healed. For I, too, am a man under authority, with soldiers under me; and I say to this one, 'Go!' and he goes; and I say to another, 'Come!' and he comes; and to my slave, 'Do this!' and he does it."

Now when Jesus heard this, He marveled at him, and turned and said to the multitude that was following Him, "I say to you, not even in Israel have I found such great faith." And when those who had been sent returned to the house, they found the slave in good health.

Luke 7:11-16

And it came about soon afterwards, that He went to a city called Nain; and His disciples were going along with Him, accompanied by a large multitude. Now as He approached the gate of the city, behold, a dead man was being carried out, the only son of his mother, and she was a widow; and a sizeable crowd from the city was with her.

And when the Lord saw her, He felt compassion for her, and said to her, "Do not weep." And He came up and touched the coffin; and the bearers came to a halt. And He said, "Young man, I say to you, arise!" And the dead man sat up, and began to speak. And Jesus gave him back to his mother. And fear gripped them all, and they began glorifying God, saying, "A great prophet has arisen among us!" and, "God has visited His people!"

Luke 7:19-23

And summoning two of his disciples, John sent them to the Lord, saying, "Are You the

Expected One, or do we look for someone else?" And when the men had come to Him, they said, "John the Baptist has sent us to You, saying, 'Are You the Expected One, or do we look for someone else?'
At that very time He cured many people of diseases and afflictions and evil spirits; and He granted sight to many who were blind. And He answered and said to them, "Go and report to John what you have seen and heard: the BLIND RECEIVE SIGHT, the lame walk, the lepers are cleansed, and the deaf hear, the dead are raised up, the POOR HAVE THE GOSPEL PREACHED TO THEM. And blessed is he who keeps from stumbling over Me."

Luke 8:41-56

And behold, there came a man named Jairus, and he was an official of the synagogue; and he fell at Jesus' feet, and began to entreat Him to come to his house; for he had an only daughter, about twelve years old, and she was dying. But as He went, the multitudes were pressing against Him. And a woman who had a hemorrhage for twelve years, and could not be healed by anyone, came up behind Him, and touched the fringe of His cloak; and immediately her hemorrhage stopped.
And Jesus said, "Who is the one who touched Me!" And while they were all

45

denying it, Peter said, "Master, the multitudes are crowding and pressing upon You."
But Jesus said, "Someone did touch Me, for
I was aware that power had gone out of
Me." And when the woman saw that she
had not escaped notice, she came trembling
and fell down before Him, and declared in
the presence of all the people the reason
why she had touched Him, and how she had
been immediately healed. And He said to
her, "Daughter, your faith has made you
well; go in peace."
While He was still speaking, someone came
from the house of the synagogue official,
saying, "Your daughter has died; do not
trouble the Teacher anymore." But when
Jesus heard this, He answered Him, "Do
not be afraid any longer; only believe, and
she shall be made well." And when He had
come to the house, He did not allow anyone
to enter with Him, except Peter and John
and James, and the girl's father and mother.
Now they were all weeping and lamenting
for her; but He said, "Stop weeping, for she
has not died, but is asleep." And they
began laughing at Him, knowing that she
had died. He, however, took her by the
hand and called, saying, "Child, arise!"
And her spirit returned, and she rose
immediately; and He gave orders for something to be given her to eat. And her parents were amazed.

Luke 9:1-6

And He called the twelve together, and gave them power and authority over all the demons, and to heal diseases. And He sent them out to proclaim the kingdom of God, and to perform healing. And He said to them, "Take nothing for your journey, neither a staff, nor a bag, nor bread, nor money; and do not even have two tunics apiece. And whatever house you enter, stay there, and take your leave from there. And as for those who do not receive you, as you go out from that city, shake off the dust from your feet as a testimony against them." And departing, they began going about among the villages, preaching the gospel, and healing everywhere.

Luke 9:37-43

And it came about on the next day, that when they had come down from the mountain, a great multitude met Him. And behold, a man from the multitude shouted out, saying, "Teacher, I beg You to look at my son, for he is my only boy, and behold, a spirit seizes him, and he suddenly screams, and it throws him into a convulsion with foaming at the mouth, and as it mauls him, it scarcely leaves him. And I begged Your disciples to cast it out, and they could not." And Jesus answered and said, "O unbelieving and perverted generation, how long

shall I be with you, and put up with you?
Bring your son here." And while he was
still approaching, the demon dashed him to
the ground, and threw him into a convul-
sion. But Jesus rebuked the unclean spirit,
and healed the boy, and gave him back to
his father.

Luke 9:56

"For the Son of Man did not come to de-
stroy men's lives, but to save them."

Luke 10:8-9

"And whatever city you enter, and they
receive you, eat what is set before you; and
heal those in it who are sick, and say to
them, 'The kingdom of God has come near
to you.'"

Luke 10:17-20

And the seventy returned with joy, saying,
"Lord, even the demons are subject to us in
Your name." And He said to them, "I was
watching Satan fall from heaven like light-
ning. Behold, I have given you authority to
tread upon serpents and scorpions, and
over all the power of the enemy, and noth-
ing shall injure you. Nevertheless do not
rejoice in this, that the spirits are subject to
you, but rejoice that your names are record-
ed in heaven."

Luke 11:14

And He was casting out a demon, and it was dumb; and it came about that when the demon had gone out, the dumb man spoke; and the multitudes marveled.

Luke 14:1-6

And it came about when He went into the house of one of the leaders of the Pharisees on the Sabbath to eat bread, that they were watching Him closely. And there, in front of Him was a certain man suffering from dropsy. And Jesus answered and spoke to the lawyers and Pharisees, saying, "Is it lawful to heal on the Sabbath, or not?" But they kept silent. And He took hold of him, and healed him, and sent him away. And He said to them, "Which one of you shall have a son or an ox fall into a well, and will not immediately pull him out on the Sabbath day?" And they could make no reply to this.

Luke 17:11-19

And it came about while He was on the way to Jerusalem, that He was passing between Samaria and Galilee. And as He entered a certain village, ten leprous men who stood at a distance met Him; and they raised their voices, saying, "Jesus, Master, have mercy on us!" And when He saw them, He said to them, "Go and show yourselves to the priests."

And it came about that as they were going, they were cleansed. Now one of them, when he saw that he had been healed, turned back, glorifying God with a loud voice, and he fell on his face at His feet, giving thanks to Him. And he was a Samaritan.

And Jesus answered and said, "Were there not ten cleansed? But the nine—where are they? Was no one found who turned back to give glory to God, except this foreigner?" And He said to him, "Rise, and go your way; your faith has made you well."

Luke 18:35-42

And it came about that as He was approaching Jericho, a certain blind man was sitting by the road, begging. Now hearing a multitude going by, he began to inquire what this might be. And they told him that Jesus of Nazareth was passing by. And he called out, saying, "Jesus, Son of David, have mercy on me!" And those who led the way were sternly telling him to be quiet; but he kept crying out all the more, "Son of David, have mercy on me!"

And Jesus stopped and commanded that he be brought to Him; and when he had come near, He questioned him, "What do you want Me to do for you?" And he said, "Lord, I want to regain my sight." And

Jesus said to him, "Receive your sight; your faith has made you well."

John 4:46-53

He came therefore again to Cana of Galilee where He had made the water wine. And there was a certain royal official, whose son was sick at Capernaum. When he heard that Jesus had come out of Judea into Galilee, he went to Him, and was requesting Him to come down and heal his son; for he was at the point of death. Jesus therefore said to him, "Unless you people see signs and wonders, you simply will not believe." The royal official said to Him, "Sir, come down before my child dies." Jesus said to him, "Go your way; your son lives."
The man believed the word that Jesus spoke to him, and he started off. And as he was now going down, his slaves met him, saying that his son was living. So he inquired of them the hour when he began to get better. They said therefore to him, "Yesterday at the seventh hour the fever left him." So the father knew that it was at that hour in which Jesus said to him, "Your son lives"; and he himself believed, and his whole household.

John 6:2

And a great multitude was following Him, because they were seeing the signs which He was performing on those who were sick.

John 9:1-7

And as He passed by, He saw a man blind from birth. And His disciples asked Him, saying, "Rabbi, who sinned, this man or his parents, that he should be born blind?" Jesus answered, "It was neither that this man sinned, nor his parents; but it was in order that the works of God might be displayed in him. We must work the works of Him who sent Me, as long as it is day; night is coming, when no man can work. While I am in the world, I am the light of the world." When He had said this, He spat on the ground, and made clay of the spittle, and applied the clay to his eyes, and said to him, "Go, wash in the pool of Siloam" ...And so he went away and washed, and came back seeing.

John 10:30
Jesus said, *"I and the Father are one."*

They are in agreement. They think the same way and they do the same things. If God is a healer, then Jesus is a healer. In John, chapter 1, it says that God and the Word are the same, and that Jesus is the Word.

Psalm 107:20

He sent His word and healed them, and delivered them from their destructions.

Hebrews 13:8

Jesus Christ is the same yesterday and today, yes and forever.

John 10:10

"The thief [Satan] comes only to steal, and kill, and destroy; I came that they might have life, and might have it abundantly."

James 1:17

Every good thing bestowed and every perfect gift is from above, coming down from the Father of lights, with whom there is no variation, or shifting shadow.

It is God's will for all of us to be healed. God has shown us this throughout His Word.

3 John 2 (KJV)

*Beloved, I wish above all things that thou mayest **prosper** and be in **health,** even as **thy** soul prospereth.*

As your soul prospers in the Word of God— as you begin to see yourself as God sees you— healing will begin to manifest itself in your body.

We must open our eyes to the Word of God, for He only sees the price already paid. It's time for you and me to receive that price. We must reach out by faith—faith in His Word. Just as we reached out in faith and took hold of His Word for salvation, for forgiveness of our sin, believing that He died on the cross for our sins, we must also believe that by His stripes we are healed.

1 Peter 2:24

He Himself bore our sins in His body on the cross, that we might die to sin and live to righteousness; for by His wounds you were healed.

Isaiah 53:5

*But He was pierced through for our trans-gressions, **He** was crushed for our iniqui-ties: the chastening of our well-being fell upon Him, and by His scourging **we** are healed.*

Exodus 23:25-26

*"But **you** shall serve the Lord your God, and He will bless **your** bread and **your** water; and I will remove sickness from your midst. There shall be no one miscarrying or barren in your land."*

Psalm 103:1-5

Bless the Lord, O my soul; and all that is within me, bless His holy name. Bless the Lord, O my soul, and forget none of His benefits.

You see, there are benefits in serving God.

[He] *pardons all your iniquities;*

[He] *heals all your diseases;*

[He] *redeems your life from the pit;*

[He] *crowns you with lovingkindness and compassion;*

[He] *satisfies your years with good things, so that your youth is renewed like the eagle.*

Jesus will not refuse to heal you. Healing is the Children's bread. Healing has been provided; it's a gift for you and me to accept.

Mark 1:39-42

He went into their synagogues throughout all Galilee, preaching and casting out the demons. And a leper came to Him, beseeching Him and falling on his knees before Him, and saying to Him, "If You are willing, You can make me clean." And moved with compassion, He stretched out His hand, and touched him, and said to him, "I am willing; be cleansed." And immediately the leprosy left him and he was cleansed.

Jesus is waiting for you, and He's waiting for me to come to Him and fall down before Him, believe His Word, and receive His healing. And I say to you today, receive the Word, for it says Jesus went about all the cities and the villages teaching in their synagogues and proclaiming the gospel of the kingdom, and He was healing every kind of sickness. **Did you hear that?** He was healing **every sickness and every disease** and He wants to heal you. So **reach out and take hold of His Word. Jesus has paid the price for you to be healed.**

Proverbs 4:20-22

My son, give attention to my words. Incline your ear to my sayings. Do not let them depart from your sight; keep them in the midst of your heart. For they are life to those who find them, and health to all their whole body.

Hebrews 11:1

Now faith is the assurance of things hoped for, the conviction of things not seen.

Hebrews 11:6

Without faith it is impossible to please Him, for he who comes to God must believe that He is, and that He is a rewarder of those who seek Him.

1 John 5:4

For whatever is born of God overcomes the world; and this is the victory that has overcome the world—our faith.

The victory that overcomes the world is our faith in the Word of God, our faith in the One

who created heaven and earth, and our faith in Jesus.

For John 10:10 tells us that Jesus has given us life and that He has given it to us abundantly. Now it's up to you and me to reach out and take hold of that life. For He wants us to walk in **His Word.** He wants us to be strengthened.

Matthew 9:20-22

Behold, a woman who had been suffering from a hemorrhage for twelve years, came up behind Him saying to herself, "If I only touch His garment, I shall get well." But Jesus turning and seeing her said, "Daughter, take courage: your faith has made you well."

Her faith was in Jesus. We must place our faith in Jesus and His Word. He and His Word are the same. And His Word says, *"By His stripes you are healed."* So let us reach out and take hold of Jesus; reach out and take hold of His Word. He is no respecter of persons.

Acts 10:34 (KJV)

Peter said, *Of a truth I perceive that God is no respecter of persons.*

Jesus reached out and touched hundreds and hundreds of people, and He made them whole. Today He is still reaching out and touching hundreds and hundreds of people and making them whole. The Word says He has healed every disease and every sickness.

We have confirmation of eight people healed of AIDS under our ministry. That which the world says cannot be healed, He has healed. You see, Jesus is the creator of heaven and earth and all that is therein. And He desires for you to be healed. He desires for us to believe His Word.

He tells us in Mark 16, that some will believe and some will not. He said those who believe shall receive salvation. And *salvation*, as we learned earlier, means "to be made whole, to be forgiven of our sin, to be made complete in Jesus." Jesus paid the complete price that you and I could be made whole.

He hung on the cross and He died for our sins, but He also bore that which was needful for us to have peace. *And by His stripes, you are healed.*

Jesus is the same, yesterday, and today, and forever.

He wants you healed.

He wants you set free.

Reach out and take hold of the Word of God.

Reach out and take hold of His promises.

His promises are for you and they are for me.

He said He's not a respecter of Jew or Gentile.

His Word is the same for each one of us.

The woman at the well believed that if she touched the hem of His garment, she would be made whole.

Whoever touches God by believing in His Word WILL BE HEALED.

The centurion made a point of contact. He said, "If You speak the Word only, my servant shall be healed." And he was healed.

Jairus made a point of contact. He said, "If You will come and lay Your hands on my daughter, she shall live and she shall be healed."

Each one of them believed that Jesus **could do it,** and when He said, "I will," they believed it was done.

We are not denying that you have sickness. We are not denying that you have pain. But according to God's Word, as far as God is concerned, the price is paid. If we will reach out and receive His Word, He says we are healed. Our bodies must line up with His Word. I choose to believe the Word of God, for He said He cannot lie.

He said, "I cannot lie." His Word tells us, *"by His stripes you are healed."* So because He cannot lie, be healed in the name of Jesus—**today!**

"I command you, today, be healed in the name of Jesus; receive your healing.

I speak the Word of God to you and say, by the stripes Jesus bore, you are healed.

I speak to every symptom that has come upon your body, and I command your body to be made whole and to be made complete.

And I command you this day, rise up.

You shall not die, you shall live.

Rise up. You shall live and not die.

I command every part of you, from the top of your head to the bottom of your feet, to be healed.

I command sickness and disease to leave you.

I command demonic spirits to turn you loose.

In the name of Jesus, I command you to be made whole.

Satan, who do you think you are?

You have no authority and no power over the believer.

You have nothing in common with the children of God.

I command you now, leave them, leave them.

I command you to let go of their bodies, for they are healed by the stripes Jesus bore.

And I speak to you, and I command you to go.

Bodies, I speak to you. Listen.

I command your bodies to be whole.

I command new parts to be made.

I command new eyes to see.

I command new ears to hear.

I command hearts to be renewed and to be strengthened.

I command you to have a new heart of flesh and not a heart of stone; a new heart of flesh, of love, of joy, of peace.

I command you to be made whole.

I command unforgiveness to leave you.

I command unforgiveness, bitterness, anger, and jealousy to leave you.

In the name of Jesus, I set you free this day, and I command you to receive God's Word that has made you whole.

For today is your day—today you are healed.
Receive it today and not tomorrow.
For you are made whole by the stripes Jesus bore.
By the stripes Jesus bore, you are made whole.
In Jesus' name."

Now I speak to you today and I say, "Listen to this Word. Get it into your spirit." For as you read and hear God's Word, faith will rise up inside of you. People who are reading this book will rise out of their wheelchairs, and many will be healed of incurable diseases. Those listening and those who are hearing the Word of God are beginning to realize what God is saying. **By His stripes they are healed.** So they are believing and receiving from God.

Receive the promise of God. He has told us that if we ask Him anything, in the name of Jesus, that He would give it to us, that our joy may be full.

In the name of Jesus, receive your healing.
Receive your healing and rise up off your bed.
Rise up now. Do something you couldn't do.
Reach out and take hold of your healing.
Reach out and take hold of the Word of God.
For today is the day of your salvation.
Today is the day of your healing.
Today is your day, not tomorrow.
For if it is tomorrow it will not come.
Today, God says, is the day of your healing.
Reach out and take hold of the price Jesus paid.
Believe on the Word of God, and **rise up.**

I command you, **Rise up** and walk. **Rise up** without pain.

I command all pain to leave, in the name of Jesus. For you are the healed of the Lord.

Today is your day.

Today the Lord has made you new.

Today He has paid the price that you could be set free.

Satan no longer has control over your body.

Now line your body up with the Word of God.

Speak to your body.

Say, "Body, I am healed. Body, rise up and walk. Body, you are strong."

For God said to **speak** to the mountain in Mark 11:23,24. **Speak** to the mountain.

Speak to that problem and tell it how big your God is and command it to leave, for you have the authority in the name of Jesus. You are healed. Now rise up, I command you, in Jesus' name.

This book has been produced to give you a new vision. You must see yourself as God sees you. You must see yourself healed, whole, out of your wheelchair, without pain, because of the price Jesus paid. As you hear the Word of God, let your faith rise up. As you hear this prayer, reach out and take hold of your healing. Read this book out loud, over and over and over again and get the Word of God into your spirit. For the Word of God will change you. **The Word of God will bring life to your flesh.**

God said to meditate on His Word day and night and it will become health to your flesh.

Now let this Word rise up in your spirit. Read it before you are prayed for, before you call for the elders. Listen to the Word of God and receive it. In the name of Jesus, let this become life to you, for life is in the Word of God.

Have You Accepted Christ?

If you have read this book and you are not sure that you have been born again, or if you have never **personally** asked Jesus to come into your life and forgive you of your sins, I invite you to pray the following prayer with me. According to Romans 10:9-13, you must personally ask God to forgive you of your sins. No one can do this for you.

Romans 10:9-13

If you confess with your mouth Jesus as Lord, and believe in your heart that God raised Him from the dead, you shall be saved; for with the heart man believes, resulting in righteousness, and with the mouth he confesses, resulting in salvation. For the Scripture says, "WHOEVER BELIEVES IN HIM WILL NOT BE DISAP-POINTED." For there is no distinction between Jew and Greek; for the same Lord is Lord of all, abounding in riches for all who call upon Him; for "WHOEVER WILL CALL UPON THE NAME OF THE LORD WILL BE SAVED."

If you believe that Jesus died to pay the price for your sins and that God raised Him from the dead, **repeat this prayer with me:**

God, I am a sinner. Please forgive me of my sins. I accept Your Son, Jesus, as my

Savior, and I accept the price He paid for my sins (His blood).

Now, Father, I promise that I will read Your Word so I can find out what a Christian is like, and then I will act like a Christian. I will go to church on a regular basis—not just once or twice a year—so I can grow strong through the strength and encouragement of fellow Christians. I realize that we need each other. When I am weak, my church family will help and encourage me, and when others are weak, I will help and encourage them.

Father, because You have just forgiven me, I now forgive myself. I don't have the right to hold on to the things You have forgiven. Your Word says that my sins will never be remembered again. I thank You for this.

Father, I forgive those who have hurt me, and I ask that You also forgive them. I know they were deceived by Satan just as I was. Please send someone to tell them about Jesus so they too can become Christians. Thank You, Father. Amen.